THE PATH OF THE GREEN MAN